M000025163

Glass Enameling
Kay Bain Weiner

First Edition:
Published in the United States by Eastman Publications.

ISBN 09625663-7-3

Dedication

To Nicole and Brendan, who have yet to experience the joys of creativity.

Acknowledgments

To complete a book takes a network of special and talented people whose combined efforts made this project possible.

My deepest appreciation and admiration go to Peggy Karr, who has rekindled my love of enameling on glass.

I am indebted to Peggy Karr, Darlene Johnson and Gil Reynolds for their generous sharing of information.

A special note of gratitude go to Marci Fourre, Anne Nodes, Ann Valsasina, Inge Lincoln, and Kathy Torpey for their untiring assistance.

My devotion goes to my husband, Herb, and my family, whose encouragement and loving support allow me the opportunity to pursue my passion for writing.

Credits

Patterns by Kay Bain Weiner, Anne Nodes and Hans Walther.

Photographs by John McMahon and Hans Walther.

Layout design by Hans Walther.

Table of Contents

Patterns

Reference

Photo 1-1
The Cougar pattern (page 59) is an intermediate skill level project.
It can be customized with your own paint style.

Chapter 1
What Is Glass Enameling?

The wonder of glass enameling is achieved through the miraculous transformation of glass granules into shimmering pools of colorful design. This phenomenon occurs in the heat of the kiln's fire, when layers of glass and color magically become one. For centuries, glass artists have applied fire-on colorants on glass to create art objects. Today, glass enameling involves hand-decorating glass surfaces with vibrantly colored granulated glass and then firing the decorated glass in a kiln.

In recent years, there have been several excellent texts written on glass fusing and hot glass techniques (see References at the back of the book). There is, however, little information exclusively devoted to the techniques of enameling glass. To fill this void, we have here—hot off the press—a book on glass enameling. I hope it will inspire you to explore this fascinating craft and experience the joy of composing a chromatic symphony in glass.

Photo 1-2
Glass Enameling techniques involve sifting dry or painting wet enamels on glass. The above pattern is on page 40 in this book.

Pioneer Glass Fusers

My interest in glass art began in the early 1960s. It was then that I became familiar with the work of pioneer glass fusers Dorothy Larson and Kay Kinney, whose creations were exhibited in major galleries and museums. Larson created a series of small fused glass tiles which were mounted on wood and used as wall decor. Kinney was a forerunner in the development and manufacture of liquid glass enamels and a line of dish and bowl slumping molds. She devoted her life to her art, producing fusing products, as well as writing a book and a number of instructional manuals. Later on, as the proprietor of a glass and craft center and because of my interest in glass fusing, I remained a devout Kinney follower and distributed the Kay Kinney fusing products over the years.

My involvement with glass enameling and fusing became serious when I studied in New York with the prominent glass artist and designer Maurice Heaton. Well known for his extraordinary glass enameling (which he began early in 1933 and perfected over many years), Heaton formed molds out of steel and used stencils to apply designs to lighting fixtures, bowls, and dishes. We can also credit Heaton with the rejuvenation in 1947 of the process of fusing crushed crystals of enamel to the under surface of glass. Years later he adapted the technique of fusing colored enamels between as many as six layers of glass. Also noted for his stained glass windows and glass art murals, Heaton exhibited in major galleries and museums throughout the world.

I recall Heaton as a master instructor from the old school. Not only did we students have to learn to decorate glass and fire it, but we had to make our own molds. And, in those years, since glass kilns were not available, we either had to use an enameling or ceramic kiln or construct our own. It was a great experience, and I continued to work with the technique of using dry enamels for two or three years. All this happened, of course, long before we had anything like the wonderful fusible colored glass manufactured today.

New Wave of Glass

When other types of glass art, such as leaded glass, gained increasing popularity, the public's interest in plate decorating and glass enameling diminished. Large, low firing enameling kilns were unavailable to the average craftsperson. Thus fused project size had to be limited. Also, the advent of new stained glass factories in this country brought to the public a spectrum of exciting colorful glass, available in a profusion of patterns and textures. This created a whole new hobby craze that has grown impressively into a lively glass art industry.

In the mid-1970's Bullseye Glass of Oregon began producing a unique type of art glass with qualities that make it ideal for fusing. The availability of fusible compatible glass opened innovative possibilities for decorating and kiln-forming glass without the use of enamels. Interest in hot glass escalated, and kiln companies began manufacturing kilns specifically made for melting glass.

Despite the amazing advancement and versatile techniques made possible by fusible glass, however, applying enamels on glass remains a distinct and unique art form.

Resurgence of Interest

Little did I realize that my enthusiasm for glass enameling would once again emerge—fueled this time by my admiration for the accomplishments of my friend Peggy Karr. Today her name is synonymous with fused glass plates, and her designs and art objects are highly prized by collectors. She began fusing glass in 1983 and dreamed of mass-producing her enameled glassware. Through exploration and ingenuity, she refined her technique to a science. Her passion for glass enameling turned her artistry into a major manufacturing operation. Peggy Karr has brought new excitement and recognition to the process of glass enameling. Her glass art, identified by its charming, distinctive style and textured colors, has won the admiration of the most discerning contemporary glass artists.

Peggy's generosity and willingness to share her secrets with me has renewed my love for glass enameling, rekindled my old flame for this hot glass medium, and inspired me to write this book. (Photo 1-3).

The Best Is Yet To Come

Through these pages, journey with me as I explain in detail the Peggy Karr technique, and explore other enameling procedures as well. We will start with basic instructions on how to select and cut glass and then describe how to create stencils, apply enamels, prepare molds, and fire the kiln. To help you get started, there is a description of glass, other materials, equipment, and related products that you will need.

Photo 1-3
Plate design by Peggy Karr Glass.

The book also includes a selection of multi-purpose patterns ranging from simple to complex for creating plates, wall hangings, and sun catchers. You will find a variety of themes offered in the pattern section—nature, impressionistic designs, and floral and traditional holiday motifs. You can use the patterns as a guide or modify or enlarge them to suit your own unique vision. Some of the patterns are shaded to indicate what areas could be done in different colors. Also included are some patterns particularly suitable for the enamel painting technique described in Chapter 6.

Chapter 7 features safety tips and proper handling of enamels and kilns. When working with any craft material, it is advisable to follow reasonable safety measures. Be sure to read Chapter 7 before proceeding with a project.

Photo 1-4
After firing, small bubbles are characteristic of laminated powder enamels.

What To Expect

Each piece you create will be one of a kind. Even if you repeat the same pattern and technique, there will be slight variations in your completed project. An infinite variety of effects can be achieved by using different manufacturers' enamels and techniques. For instance, the dry enamel application when fired will retain a granular appearance as opposed to the painted effect of a wet enamel application.

After firing, small bubbles are not uncommon in laminated projects such as dishes and are characteristic of the medium. (Photo 1-4). The type of kiln separator or fiber paper used on the mold or shelf (see Chapter 6) will add a texture to the back of a plate or flat piece.

The desire to create something elegant, something truly special, is always present in anyone who works with their hands. Through exploration and practice you will become proficient in working with the medium.

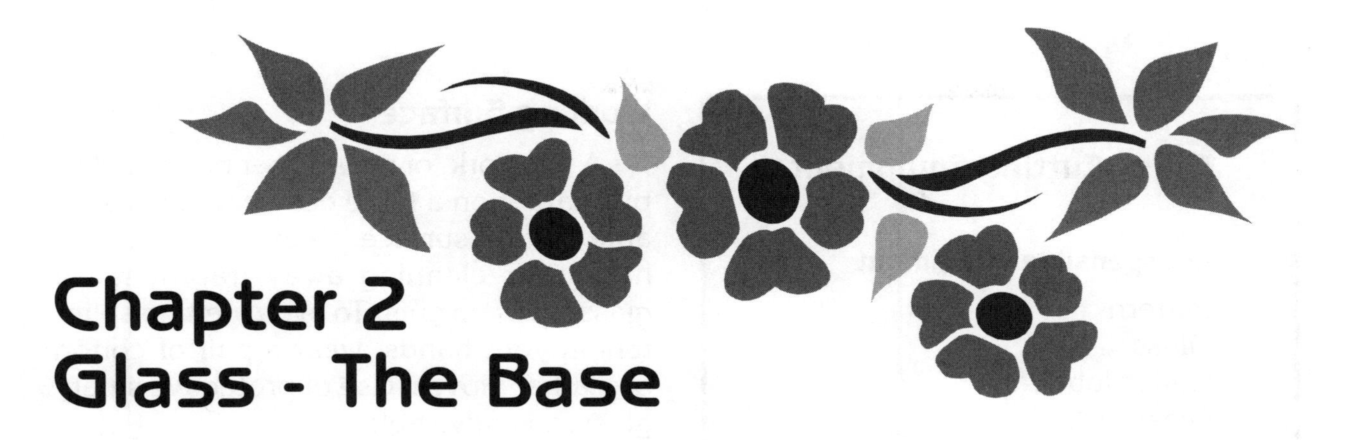

Chapter 2
Glass - The Base

Patterns and Types of Glass

Most of the stencil patterns in this book have been designed to create circular 8-inch plates using clear glass. All of the patterns can also be modified or enlarged and used on projects that are fired flat or slumped in various sizes and shapes of molds.

For most of the patterns in this book, use float glass. In recent years, much of the clear glass produced in the United States is made by a float glass process. As molten glass flows from the furnace, it floats across the surface of a bath of molten tin. The temperature is lowered as the glass moves across the tin. When the glass becomes rigid, it leaves the tin surface to pass through an annealing oven. The result is a smooth sheet of glass with two completely different surfaces. The tin side of the glass can discolor when fused with enamel glass colors.

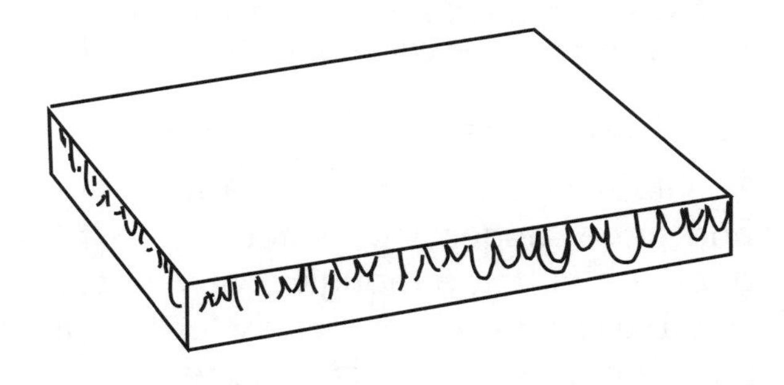

Illustration 2-1
This enlarged view shows the ragged edge of the tin side of float glass.

Tin Side of Glass

You can identify the tin side by examining the cut edge of the glass through a magnifying glass or by using a special light. Examine the side where the glass has been cut, and you will see that the tin side has tiny ridges on one edge. (Rolled or sheet glass - non-tinned - is ideal to work with but is not readily available. (Illustration 2-1).

Purchasing Glass

You can buy float glass through glass shops. For most projects under 8 inches, two pieces of single-thick clear float glass are suitable. For larger projects, use double-thick clear glass. After fusing, the lamination of two double-thick pieces of glass is equivalent to a 1/4-inch thickness.

Colored Glass

Colored glass can be used to create enamel projects. Be sure to purchase glass marked fusible, both for the colored glass and for the clear top glass, if you are laminating.

Glass Cutting Equipment

Indispensible Equipment

Pattern
Glass
Cutter lubricant
Glass cutter
Running pliers
Grozing/Breaking pliers

Safety Suggestions

Safety glasses
Gloves
Table brush

Optional Equipment

Glass marking pen
Ruler
T-square
Circle cutter

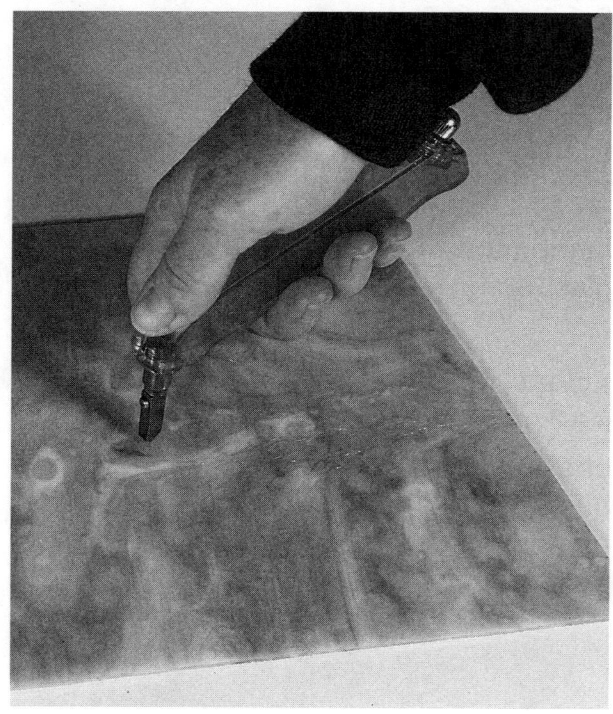

Photo 2-1
A pistol grip cutter is easy to use for a beginner.

Working Surface

A felt, cork, or newspaper pad or a flat-pile carpet on a table can serve as a suitable cutting surface. Keep a small brush handy for cleaning away fragments of glass between cuts. To avoid getting splinters in your hands, wear a pair of cotton or leather gloves. Use of protective safety glasses is advisable.

How Glass Is Cut

With little effort, you can cut glass by scribing or scoring the smooth surface with a rotating cutter wheel and separating the glass on the score line. Rolling a cutter wheel with consistent pressure over the surface creates fissures that fracture the glass to a minimum depth. The glass is then separated on the score line by using your hands or pliers. (Illustration 2-2).

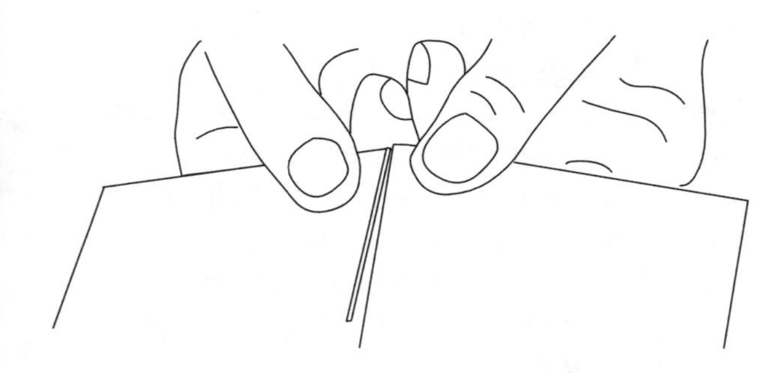

Illustration 2-2
To break glass apart after scoring, thumbs should be placed on either side of the score line.

Pistol Grip Cutter

Glass cutters come in various types and price ranges.The pistol grip self-lubricating cutter, although costly, is comfortable to control, especially for a beginner. The entire hand is wrapped around the handle. The carbide wheel is very durable but can be replaced easily if necessary. (Photo 2-1).

Standard Glass Cutters

The standard steel wheel cutter and the carbide wheel cutter can be held in different ways. Find the position that is most comfortable for you. Many professionals hold the cutter between the first and second fingers. The thumb supports the cutter on the underside. When the teeth of the cutter are down, the wheel is visible, and you can guide the cutter along the pattern lines. (Illustration 2-4).

In another cutting position, the cutter handle is tucked into the fold of the palm. Press your index finger on top of the flat shoulder of the cutter, and place your thumb along the side of the handle. (Illustration 2-5).

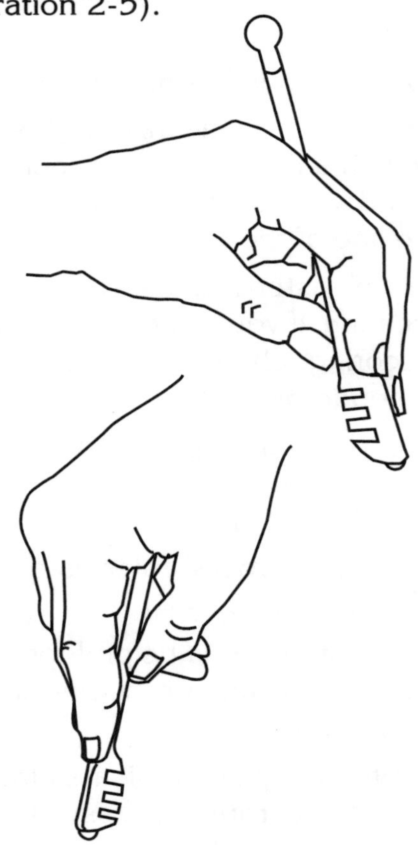

Illustrations 2-4 & 5

Indispensable Tools

Running Pliers

Running pliers are most successful on straight or gently curved lines, provided there is at least 1/2 inch of glass on each side of the score line. Align the center mark on the top of the pliers directly on the score line (at the spot where the cut ends). Squeeze the handles so that the jaws (nose) of the pliers exert even pressure on either side of the score, and run the break line. (Photo 2-2).

The set screw on the top of the pliers can be adjusted, if necessary, to accommodate the thickness of the glass. (Illustration 2-6)

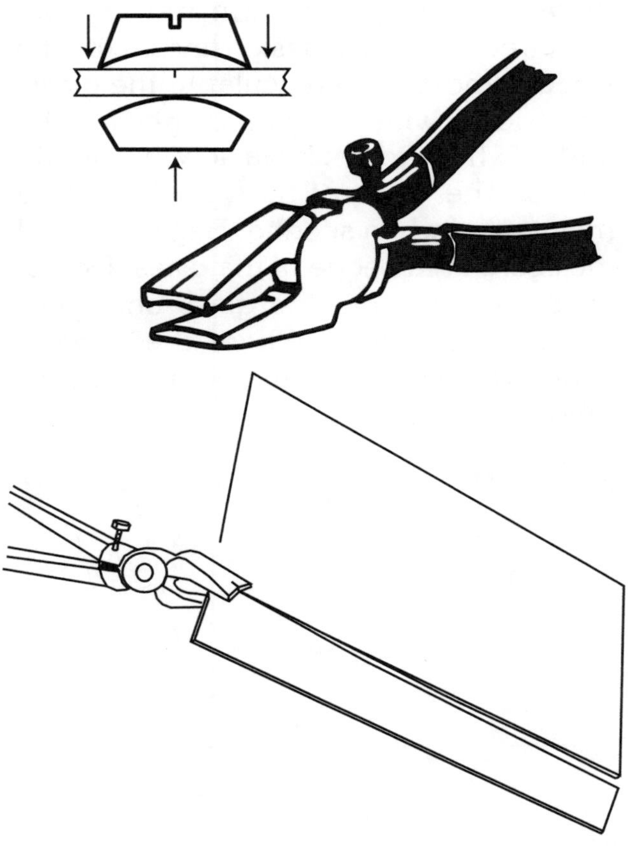

Illustration 2-6
Running pliers will create a run in the scored glass. The set screw as seen above can be adjusted to accommodate the thickness of the glass.

Breaking Pliers

Breaking pliers are invaluable for removing pieces of glass too small to grasp by hand. Place the jaws of the pliers parallel to the score line where the score ends (where it is "hottest"). These pliers can be used to break away narrow strips or curved pieces by pulling away and down on the score line.

General Cutting Techniques

Position

For the best arm leverage to cut glass, stand at a table whose top is between 34 inches and 36 inches from the floor. For proper scoring pressure and speed, use the weight of your entire arm, moving your wrist freely to follow design lines. With the wheel almost perpendicular to the glass, bear down with enough weight for the cutter wheel to make a low humming sound. The angle of the wheel must be maintained when scoring. Begin and end the score at the edge of the glass. Do not lift the cutter from the glass until your score is complete. Where the scoring ended will be the starting point for separation. (Illustration 2-7).

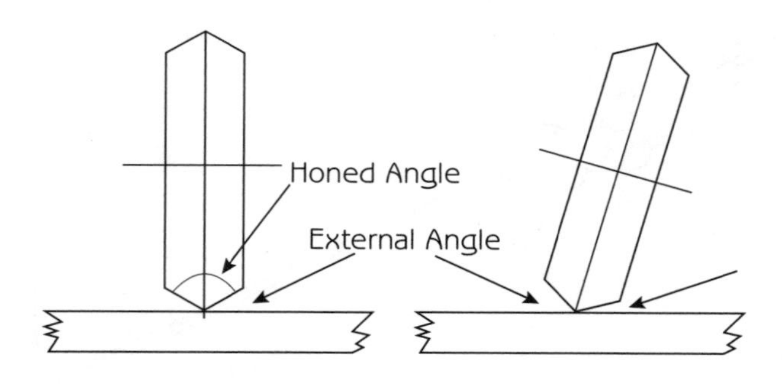

Illustration 2-7
The cutter must not lean sideways. If it does, then the sides of the wheel will bear against the sides of the fissure and result in partial skidding.

If you are not using a self-lubricating cutter, dip the cutter wheel into lubricant before each cut. Keep some liquid lubricant in a small jar with steel wool or a cut sponge at the bottom.

Scoring

For straight (or curved) cuts, your cutter wheel can be drawn either toward you or away from you. To prevent the wheel from getting caught on the edge of the glass, start 1/16 inch away from the edge.

Important: Separate glass immediately after scoring, while the score lines are still "hot".

Suggestions

❍ Never use a dull or damaged cutter.

❍ Before cutting, clean the glass thoroughly with a liquid glass cleaner or ammonia and water so that nothing interferes with the line of the cut.

❍ Use consistent pressure and speed when scoring. If you do not hear the sound of the scoring, chances are you are not using enough pressure.

❍ Never go over a cut line twice. If your score is not successful, start a new cut line in a different spot.

❍ Use a heavy metal ruler as a cutting guide for straight lines.

❍ A T-square ruler is helpful for cutting straight lines because it hooks onto the edge of a table.

❍ A white, gritty line indicates that you have used too much pressure or not enough lubricant. The score line should be a faint visible line with an oil trail.

Separating a Straight, Large Piece

A straight cut on a large piece of glass can be broken along the edge of a table. Place the glass so that the score line is parallel to the edge of the table and extends slightly over the table's edge. While pressing one hand firmly on the portion of glass on the table, use the other hand, with your thumb on top of the extended portion, to snap the glass with a motion down and away, similar to snapping scored saltine crackers.

Separating a Strip of Glass

Another way to break a straight line score (no narrower than 1 inch wide) is to wedge a ruler under one end of the score line. Press evenly with a thumb on each side of the score line near the ruler, causing a run to follow along the score. (Illustration 2-8).

To break away a narrow strip of glass, hold the glass with a thumb on each side of the score line, and gently bend the glass so that it will break apart. Another method is to place breaking glass pliers perpendicular to the glass and against the end of the score line, where the score is "hottest". Then pull the glass away with the pliers.

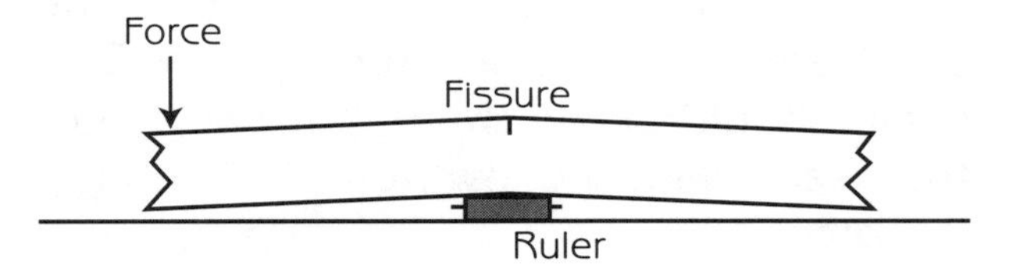

Illustration 2-8
This drawing shows one technique for separating glass. A ruler is used as a continuous support directly under the entire length of the score. It establishes a fulcrum over which the glass is bent to develop the full fracture.

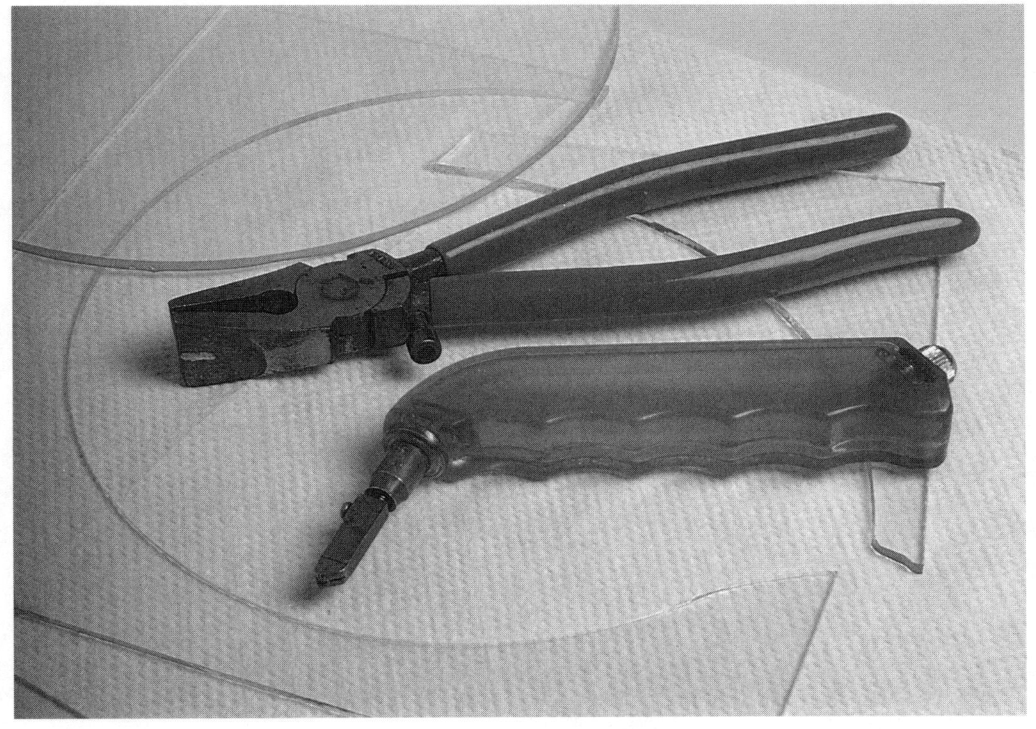

Photo 2-2
Running pliers and pistolgrip cutters are helpful tools for cutting glass. *See pages 12 & 13.*

Cutting and Separating Circles

Circle Cutters

Score glass on the non-tin side. For projects in this book, use a circle cutter capable of cutting circles up to 12 inches in diameter. Cut glass into a square at least 1 to 2 inches larger than the circle. Most circle cutters have a suction cup that holds the cutter in place.

❍ Insert the scale beam fully into the pivot and tighten the thumb screw. The scale should be on the upper surface of the beam, with the low numbered end at the pivot.

❍ Set the cutting head at the diameter you wish to cut. Read the scale at the edge of the cutting head nearest the vacuum head pivot. (Photo 2-3)

❍ Place clean glass on a flat, hard surface. Hold the pivot at the center of the circle, and activate the vacuum lever, if your cutter has one. Cross lines on the base of the pivot will help you to locate the center of the circle.

❍ With a small brush, apply a wide ring of lubricant on the glass surface.

❍ Press down on the cutting head thumb knob, and score the circle in one smooth, continuous action, stopping exactly at the starting point. Do not overlap scores.

❍ Make the lightest continuous score without flaking by adjusting the amount of pressure on the thumb knob.

❍ Turn the glass over on a pliable surface (pad of newspaper, felt, cork, or carpet), and press down with your thumbs over the scoreline. The score will run a short distance. Continue to apply pressure around the circle until the complete circle has been run. (Photo 2-4)

Photo 2-3
Circle cutters are invaluable for accurate cutting of circles.

Photo 2-4
Place the scored circle upside down on newspaper and press on score line to "run" the circle.

Illustration 2-9
After scoring the circle, cut several relief tangential lines near the scored circle. There is less likelihood of a relief cut running into the body of the shape if it is made diagonally. It is important that the relief cuts start close to the main score and are drawn to the edge of the glass.

❍ Turn the glass over again and score several tangential lines with a hand cutter. They should start 1/8 inch outside the circle and end at the edge of the glass. Do not let these score lines reach the circle. (Illustration 2-9)

❍ With glass pliers pull the glass away from the circle. (Photo 2-5)

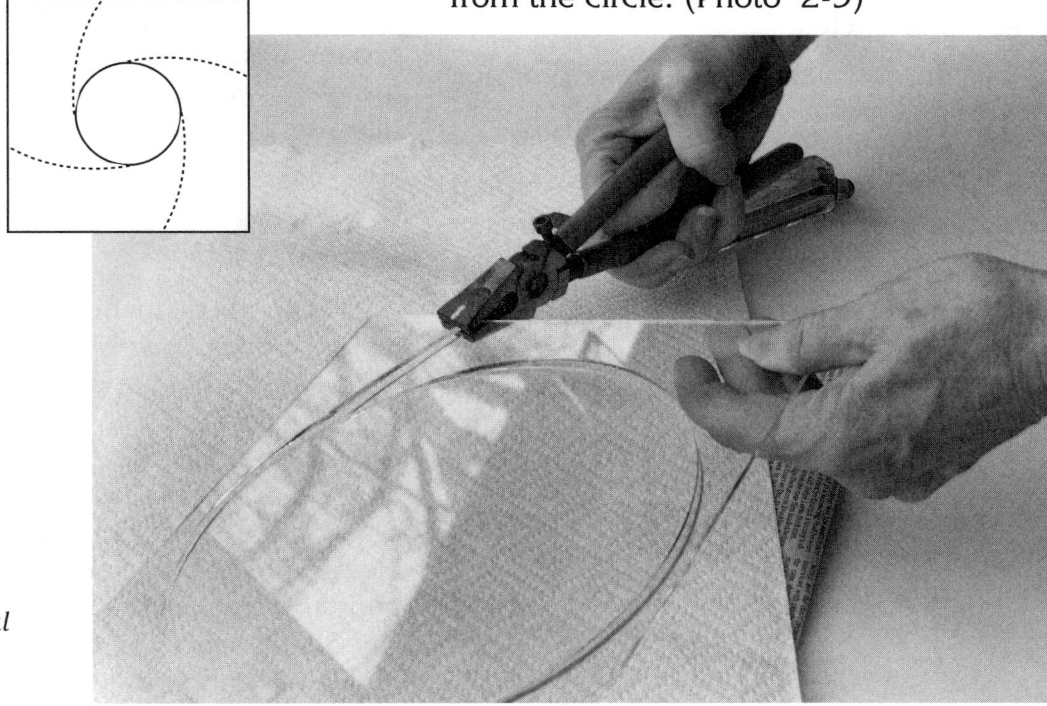

Photo 2-5
Pliers are helpful for removing excess pieces.

Photo 2-6
Sifted enamels are laminated between two single thick circles of float glass.

For later use, when you are preparing your project for firing, score a scrap of glass to create several small chips of glass 1/16 inch x 1/16 inch. A rolling pin can be used to roll out the chips from a scored piece of glass.

Free-Hand Circles

If you are planning to mass-produce dishes or circular ornaments, a circle cutter is an invaluable tool. Perfect circles are difficult to cut without a circle-cutting tool, but if you don't have one, try this:

❍ Cut the glass into a square, allowing a 1-inch to 2-inch margin around the circle pattern.

❍ Draw a small mark on the circle pattern at top and bottom. Score only a half-circle at a time.

❍ With the glass over the pattern, begin scoring from the bottom mark to the top mark. Then lift the cutter, if necessary, and score the remaining half of the circle.

❍ After scoring the circle, score several tangential relief lines from the circle to the edge of the glass (as seen in illustration 2-9). These extra cuts will enable you to break away small sections of glass without shattering the circle.

❍ With running pliers at the scored line, create a run by gently pulling down all around the circle, but do not break away the glass. After the run is visible, pull the glass away with pliers.

Cleaning Glass

Wash glass in detergent and warm water, or scrub with powdered cleanser (such as Comet) and rinse well. Dry between newspapers or with a lint-free towel. Glass can be cleaned with denatured alcohol (flammable). Don't use rubbing alcohol because it contains oils. Window cleaners are not suitable because they contain silicones that make colors crawl. Handle glass by the edges to avoid marring it with fingerprints.

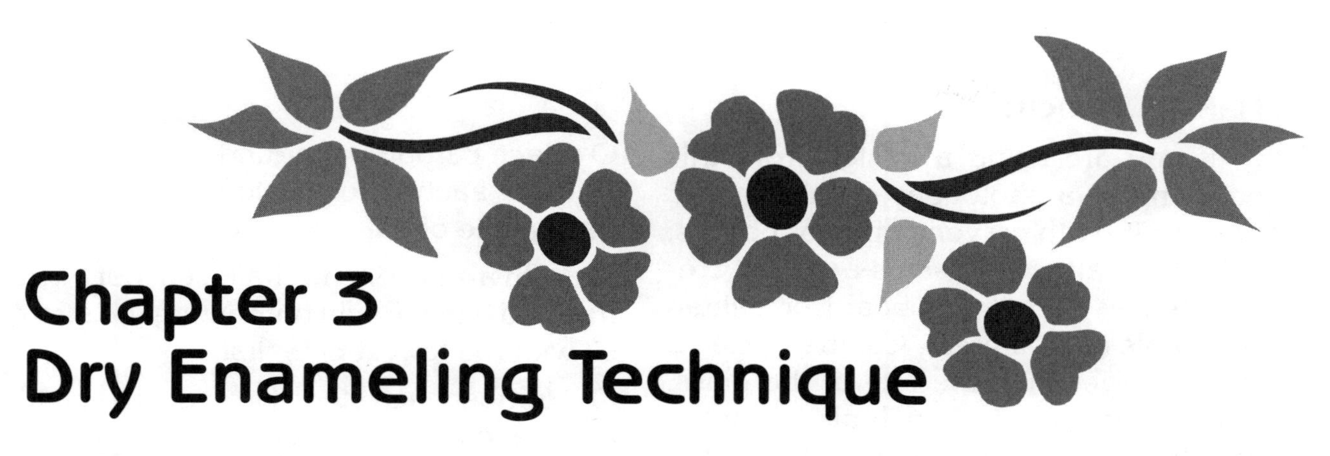

Chapter 3
Dry Enameling Technique

Enameling Supplies

Dry powdered glass enamels:
Thompson Enamel (opaque 80 mesh, medium temperature, low expansion enamels for window glass, 5000 series)
Fuse Master Enamel (by Fusion Headquarters, opaque, lead-free)
2 or 3 large sheets of oaktag or railroad board
Stencil knife
Masking tape
Carbon paper
Crayons
Kiln or mold separator
5 or 6 enameling sifters, various sizes
Wire kitchen strainer
Toothpicks
Kiln with pyrometer
Optional: light box

For the dry enamel projects in this book, it is recommended that you create stencils to sift the dry enamels onto the appropriate areas of the glass. Each color you use requires tracing and cutting a separate stencil for that color area. For example, if you are using five colors, you will need to create five stencils. A stencil can be used twice for shading a color such as a leaf. (Photo 3-1).

Photo 3-1
A separate stencil is created for each color section of the pattern. This folk art pattern requires five separate stencils.

Making Stencils

If you are using a design from this book, make a photocopy of the pattern, or trace it. With crayons or color pencils, color the pattern to use as a guide. Create stencils of railroad board or oaktag (available at art stores). Cut the oaktag 2 inches larger than the size of the glass. For instance, for an 8-inch plate, cut the oaktag into a 10-inch square. The oaktag is stiffer when it is not much larger than the plate or design size.

To make your stencils, use the following procedure:

❍ Measure the oaktag with a ruler 1/2 inch from the edge on three sides. With a sharp instrument such as a putty knife, make a scoreline. Notch out two corners, as illustrated. (Illustration 3-1)

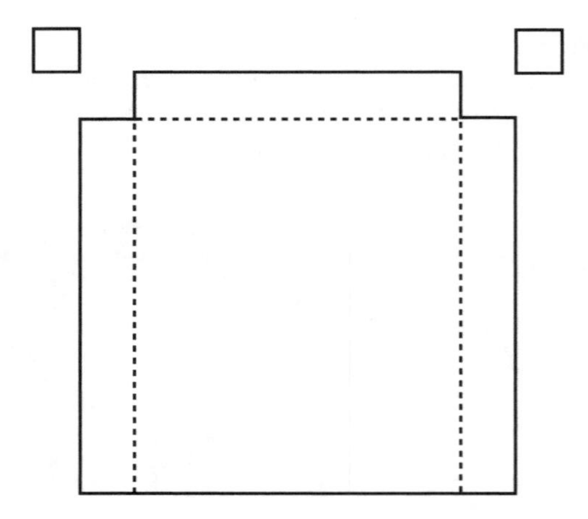

Illustration 3-1
Cut out two corners of the oaktag before folding on three sides.

❍ Save the corners to use as spacers (to be described later). Bend up the three edges and put masking tape on the three folded sides of the oaktag. This makes the oaktag easier to handle.

❍ Place carbon paper under the pattern to trace each color design section onto each piece of oaktag. (Photo 3-2)

❍ With a sharp stencil knife, cut out each traced design. Begin numbering the stencil with the fewest cuts first.

❍ Number each stencil in sequence, and mark each with the name of the color to be used. (Photo 3-3)

❍ When storing stencils for future use, place them flat, one on top of the other.

(There are also excellent stencil patterns available in Dover Books).

Using Enamels

Enamels, molds, kilns, and glass cutting tools are available at some glass suppliers and ceramic shops (see back of book for listing of products and manufacturers). Contact manufacturer for nearest dealer. Clear glass is also available at glass shops, home centers, and stained glass suppliers.

Many enamels are designed for decorating copper. However, some Thompson Enamels and Fusion Headquarters' Fuse Master enamels have an expansion rate compatible with glass. Use Thompson Enamel's opaque enamel colors, 80 mesh, or Fusion Headquarters' opaques. Enamels are sifted and fired between two layers of single-thick glass. This secures the enamels between the glass layers when fired.

For convenience, place each enamel color in its own container — a small box will do nicely. Any enamels that become mixed can be put into one container. This mixture can then be used in areas of a design where a mixed shade is desirable.

Photo 3-2
To create each stencil, use carbon paper under the pattern. Trace each color section onto its own piece of oaktag.

Photo 3-3
Cut out each traced design section with a sharp stencil knife.

Sifting Enamels

Place the colored pattern under the clear glass disk or light colored fusible glass. Use a light box, if it is available. A light box enables you to judge enamel quantities more accurately. Be sure the work surface area is clean. Apply enamel to the non-tin side of the glass (explained in Chapter 2).

❍ Carefully place stencil #1 directly over the appropriate design area. Line up the stencil by looking down and checking against the pattern.

❍ Scoop dry enamel into a small sifter. Hold the sifter in one hand, and gently tap the sifter with a knife or your finger (Photo 3-4). Note that Fuse Master enamels are finer ground than Thompson Enamels. Therefore, using a spoon or other instrument might be useful to sift the finer enamel through the mesh of the sifter. A suggestion from the manufacturer is to spray the glass surface with a small amount of hair spray prior to sifting the enamel on the desired area. This will keep the enamels intact.

❍ Put previously cut oaktag spacers (notched corners) on four edges of the glass circle. Spacers help to keep the enamel in place when the stencil is lifted. (Illustration 3-2).

Illustration 3-2
Cut pieces of oaktag will keep the stencils from touching the sifted enamels.

Photo 3-4
Fill the sifter with the desired enamel color. Starting with the stencil with the fewest cuts, gently tap the side of the sifter.

Photo 3-5
Apply an even amount of enamels over the cut stencil. It is helpful to work over a light box.

Photo 3-6
To lift stencil, use two hands. Lift one side gently and then the other side.

❍ Another method of sifting Fuse Master enamel is to use a baby food jar or empty film container. Remove the top. Cut an old nylon stocking to fit the top and attach it with a rubber band. Use the container as a shaker.

❍ Cover the area with an even amount of enamel. Keep the thickness of the sifted enamels even, so that when the upper glass blank is placed on top, it will be level. (Photo 3-5)

❍ When lifting the stencil, use two hands on the masked edges. First, carefully lift one side of the stencil about an inch, and then remove the entire stencil. (Photo 3-6)

❍ After using the first stencil, put excess enamel back into its own receptacle.

❍ Repeat this procedure for each stencil with each color.

❍ When you are finished, remove the spacers.

Note: If using opaque colored glass (which you cannot see through) use a light colored carbon paper to trace the design onto the glass. Colored carbon paper is available in sewing or art stores.

Experiment with shading when you are working with patterns such as fish, leaves, water, birds, or clothing. Shading will add more interest and dimension to your completed project. To shade a particular section, the stencil you create can be used twice — first to apply the dominant color and then to sift on a small amount of a different color for shading.

When all the desired colors have been sifted onto the plate, it is time to prepare the mold.

Chapter 4
Molds and Kiln Shelves

Selecting a Mold

A good selection of glass fusing molds in various sizes and shapes is available from art glass suppliers. Flatter molds are better than deeper molds for fusing two layers of glass because the glass fuses together with fewer bubbles.

Slumping molds can be made out of ceramic greenware. Choose greenware that has a gradual curve to the sides. Drill at least three air vents into the bottom of the mold. Greenware will become durable bisque and serviceable as a glass mold when fired to 1751° F.

Preparing a Mold

If you are using two or three plate molds of the same size and shape, you can fire them in a kiln that has side heating elements. Plate stackers (available from ceramic shops) can be used in the kiln to stack two or three molds in layers. (Photo 4 -1)

A powdered mold separator or kiln wash sifted onto the mold will prevent the glass from adhering to it. A large cardboard box can serve as a sifting area. Do not coat molds near decorated projects because particles of the separator can adhere to them.

Photo 4-1
A kiln with side elements can be used to stack two or three plate molds

❍ Stick toothpicks into the air holes of the mold to prevent them from filling with mold separator.

❍ Use a wire kitchen strainer to sift kiln separator over the mold, and evenly cover the bottom. (A small piece of chain placed in the strainer with the dry kiln separator will help break up any lumps and distribute a more even coat of separator.) (Photo 4-2)

❍ Remove the toothpicks.

❍ Place the decorated project on the mold. Holding the decorated glass by the edges, center it on the mold. Place four tiny clean glass chips (described in Chapter 2) around the edge of the plate. (Illustration 4-1). This will allow the air to dissipate during firing. Carefully place the second piece of washed glass on top of the decorated piece. Remember to place the glass tin side down. (Photo 4- 3).

Illustration 4-1
Small glass chips should be placed between the two layers of glass before firing.

Preparing the Kiln Shelf

If you are making a flat panel or jewelry, it can be fired on a kiln shelf. A kiln shelf must be coated with kiln wash, or covered with ceramic fiber paper to prevent the glass from sticking to the shelf. If the kiln shelf has been used before, scrape off all the old kiln wash with a putty knife or plastic scrubbing pad. Wear a dust mask to keep from inhaling particles.

Kiln wash can be mixed as follows: Use one part dry powder to one part water. Mix to the consistency of light cream.

Use a soft bristle brush (hake brush) to apply three or four coats of kiln wash. Load the brush and apply an even horizontal coat over the entire surface. Wait a few minutes and then apply a vertical second coat. Repeat procedure for the next two coats. Allow the kiln shelf to air dry completely or place it in a warm kiln at 500° F for an hour or two.

Devitrification

Devitrification is the formation of minute crystals over a certain time and temperature, making the glass appear hazy or giving it a matte finish. This sometimes occurs during the fusing process in the temperature range of 1350° F to 1600° F. To eliminate devitrification, brush or airbrush a liquid glass over-glaze such as Fusion's Super Spray on the top piece of glass. To discourage devitrification if not using Super Spray, fire the kiln on the highest setting to pass quickly through this temperature range. (See firing procedure in Chapter 5.)

Photo 4-2
To apply kiln wash on the mold, use a strainer to evenly sift the powder. The toothpicks are inserted in the air holes during sifting and then removed.

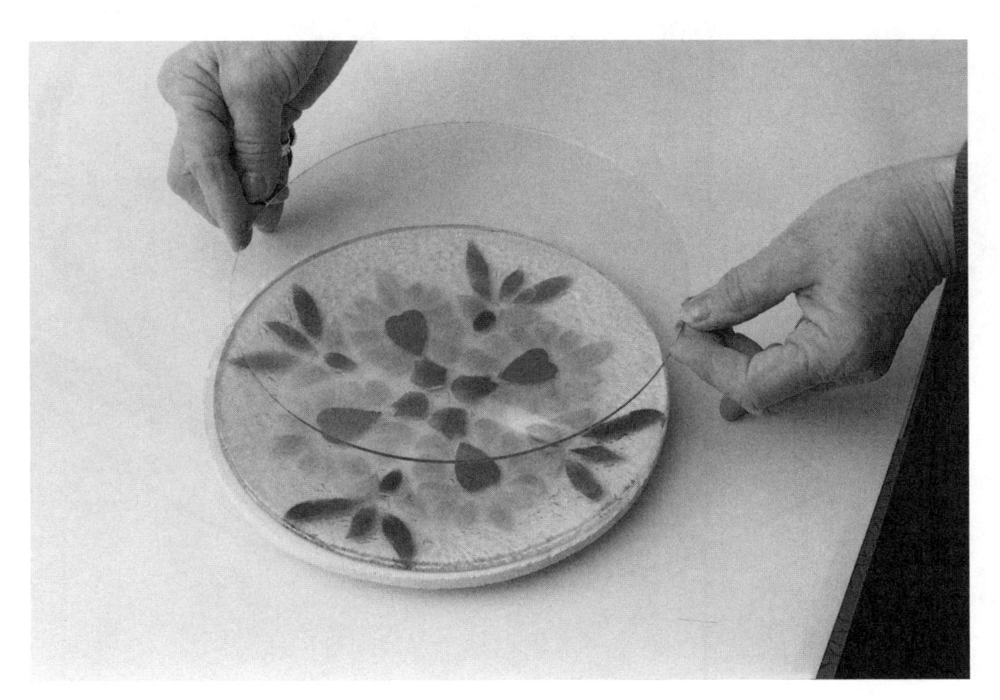

Photo 4-3
Center the decorated glass circle onto the mold. Place the top piece of glass directly over the first piece.

Abstract Pattern

This pattern can be painted with liquid enamel or you can create stencils for siftting dry enamels.

Chapter 5
Kiln Firing

Back at the Kiln. . .

To mature (melt) enamels, laminate layers of glass, or slump glass into molds, a kiln is required. Enamels mature at a temperature of 1250° F to 1479° F. Laminating layers of glass and slumping require a firing temperature of 1500° F to 1600° F, when the glass and enamels become one and take the shape of the mold.

If you are using a kiln that has only top heating elements, stacking or layering kiln shelves is not advisable. If the kiln has elements on the sides, you can fire two or possibly three layers, depending on the height of the kiln. (Photo 5-1)

Keep notes on your firing schedule so that they can be used for future reference.

Photo 5-1
The plates shown in the photo have been fired in a kiln that has top heating elements. The above designs are available in the pattern section of this book.

For convenience, use a kiln that has a pyrometer – a temperature-measuring device. All kilns are not created equal. Some have hot spots with which you will become familiar. Occasionally, a pyrometer will be inaccurate and will need to be calibrated (adjusted). You can check the accuracy of your pyrometer by placing a pyrometric cone in your kiln when firing. Cones are pyramids of clay and minerals that soften and bend at various specific temperatures For instance, a large 018 cone will bend at 1285° F to 1323° F. An 014 cone bends at 1533° F to 1540° F. (Illustration 5-1)

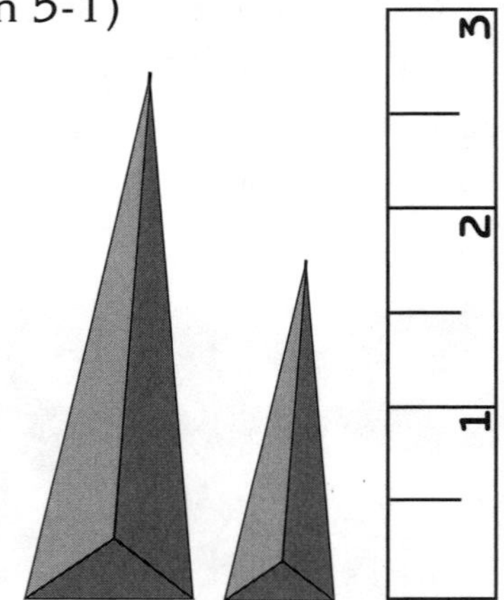

Illustration 5-1
Cones come in various sizes and gauge the temperature in the kiln by bending at specific temperatures.

If you are creating flat projects such as sun catchers, a generous coating of kiln wash should be used to keep the glass from fusing onto the kiln shelf. As an alternative to the kiln wash, use ceramic fiber shelf paper, which comes in various thicknesses. Cut the shelf paper to size and fire it in your kiln to 1300° F before using it under your project. The paper gives off fumes when fired, so it is necessary to ventilate the kiln during firing. Fiber shelf paper lasts for several firings if handled carefully.

Ready, Aim, Fire. . .

If you are inexperienced at operating a kiln, fire a few test pieces.

❍ Start the kiln on low with the peephole open or the door slightly ajar until the pyrometer reads 500° F. Allowing the kiln to vent at this point slows down the heating process, minimizing the possibility of thermal shock. Venting will also allow glue fumes or other gaseous materials to leave the kiln and not contaminate the surface of the glass.

❍ Close the peephole or door at 500° F.

❍ When the temperature reaches 700° F, turn the control dial to medium until it reaches 1000° F. At 1000° F, turn the control dial to high.

❍ Fire until the pyrometer reaches 1550° F, or until two pieces of glass have rounded and become one. You can safely peek in and check the firing process once the kiln has reached 1200° F. The glass will appear shiny and wet when it is in the process of fusing.

❍ Turn off the kiln.

❍ Open the kiln peephole and door to flash cool to 1100° F. This stops the heating process. Once the kiln has been cooled to 1100° F, close the door and peephole and allow the kiln to cool naturally.

Glass Melting Stages

Here is the cycle of changes that occurs in the glass at various temperatures:

❍ 1000° F to 1350° F, float glass remains a rigid blank, although it is expanding invisibly.

❍ From 1350° F to 1400° F, float glass starts rounding at the edges and sags slightly. The opaque enamels mature but can be fired to 1550° F.

❍ From 1400° F to 1450° F, float glass may be completely bent, or very nearly so, depending on its hardness and the type of kiln used.

❍ From 1450° F to 1550° F, depending on the kiln, float glass will be ideally sagged and laminated.

❍ Beyond 1550° F, further distortion takes place. Commercial glass forms needle-like points, and any surface colorants begin to recede from the outer edge inward.

Note: If you are using colored fusible glass, decrease the above temperatures by 50° F.

Your kiln may cool down too quickly if it is constructed of fiber or is not well insulated. Once your glass has been fused and the kiln is turned off, time the cooling rate. Begin timing after the temperature has cooled to 1000° F. The temperature should not drop faster than 2° F per minute, or about 100° F per hour. If the kiln's temperature drops more than 100°F per hour, it will be necessary to anneal the project.

Most kilns constructed of ceramic brick are well insulated and cool slowly. Therefore, smaller glass projects (8 inches and under) such as those described in this book do not need to be annealed if you are using a ceramic brick kiln.

Annealing

Annealing is the process of slowing down the cooling process through the temperature range of 1100° F to 700° F to prevent internal stress within the glass.

To anneal your projects, wait until the kiln has cooled down to 900° F. Set the kiln control on low, maintaining the temperature between 900° F and 1000° F for 1 hour. Turn off the kiln and allow it to cool naturally.

Important Firing Tips

❍ Leave the glass in the kiln to cool. *Curiosity killed the glass.* You can remove your project when the temperature reaches 300° F. But be careful — the glass will still be hot.

❍ A good rule to remember is: **Never open a kiln when its temperature is between 500° F and 1000° F during either the heating or cooling process.**

❍ To avoid excess bubbles, do not over-fuse. Under-fired glass pieces can be re-fired unless they have large bubbles.

❍ Over-firing can result in a frosted appearance on the surface of the glass. Over-firing also causes needle-like points on the edges of the glass.

❍ Dull colors indicate inaccurate firing. Check cooled project. If under-fired, re-fire to correct temperature.

Cleaning the Finished Product

After lifting the glass from the mold, clean the excess kiln separator from the fused glass. Use a brush to remove the kiln separator under running water. Discard the dry mold separator that remains on the mold, it should not be used again.

If you are using kiln ceramic fiber paper, the fibers may stick to a fired piece and should be removed with a brush under running water. This prevents the fibers from getting into the air, and you from inhaling them.

Fused dishes properly annealed are dishwasher safe.

Mushroom Garden Pattern

Painting with liquid enamel is suggested for this pattern. Refer to photo 6-1.

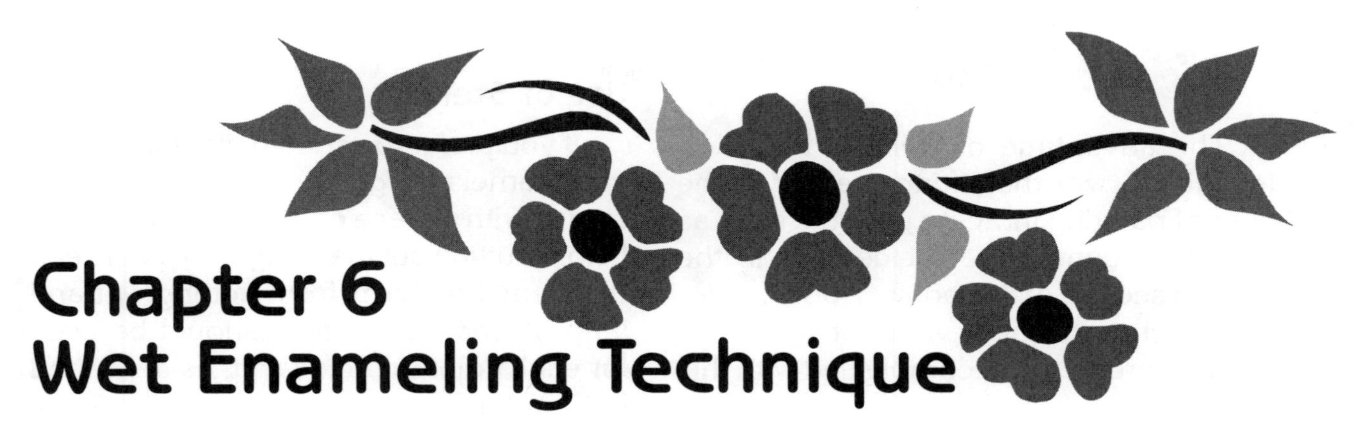

Chapter 6
Wet Enameling Technique

Liquid Enamels

In recent years, new types of enamels have become available that offer the opportunity to create different effects by applying them with an artist's brush, a sponge, a stipple brush, or an airbrush. Refer to the back of the book for manufacturers of various enamels.

The brush-on enamel technique can be accomplished by using ready-made liquid enamels, such as Unique Glass colors (to be described later) or by using Fuse Master brand enamels with a medium. Fuse Master's are powdered enamels that can be sifted as described in Chapter 3 or mixed with a medium to create a liquid enamel. These enamels can be painted on single-or double-thick glass or laminated between two single-thick pieces of glass.

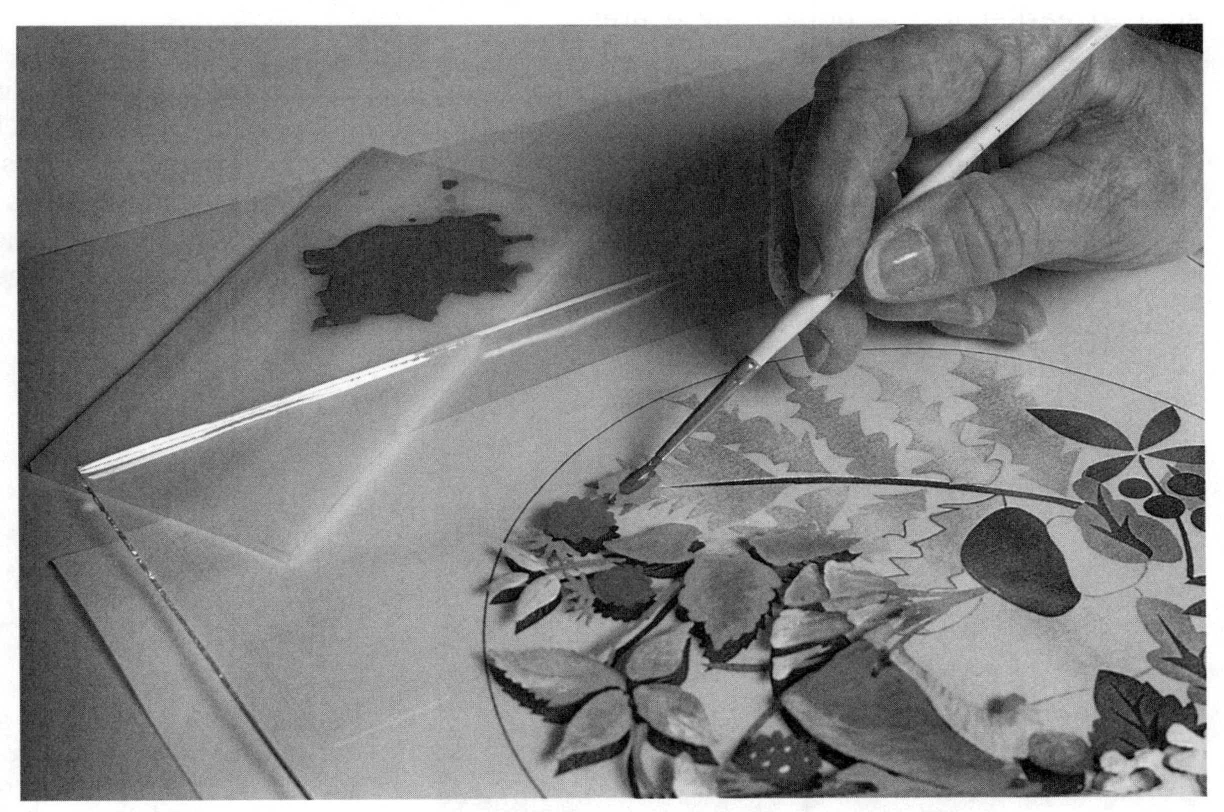

Photo 6-1
Liquid enamel is being painted and blended on transparent glass which is placed over the Mushroom Garden pattern. (See also page 32).

The advantage of a liquid brush-on technique over the sifting method is the ease of painting intricate patterns such as the mushroom or parrot designs in the pattern section of this book. Applying details such as a face, veins of a leaf, or shading are easily accomplished with this method.

When using a painting technique, it is not necessary to create stencils. By placing a colored pattern under the clear glass, you can easily see the design, so you can paint and blend the colors directly on the glass. (Photo 6-1). It is helpful to use a light box when painting because it enables you to apply the liquid enamels evenly.

To create a plate using liquid enamels, laminate the enamels between two layers of clear glass in the manner described earlier in the book. There are drape molds available that can be used for a food-safe piece, if you prefer to use a single piece of glass. The enamel will be on the underside of the plate. (Photo 6-2).

Use of Stencils

If you prefer to use stencils while painting enamels on glass, cover each paper stencil with a piece of clear contact paper before cutting out the design. This will keep the stencil patterns from getting wet and limp. A separate stencil should be used for each color in the design, as described in Chapter 3.

When using stencils, apply wet enamels with a stencil brush (a stiff blunt-cut brush). Load the brush with the enamel. Use a straight up-and-down dabbing motion until the area is completely filled.

Commercially made plastic stencils can also be used. (Stencil brushes and stencils are available in paint stores and craft shops.)

Preparing the Glass

Clean glass by scrubbing with detergent and water or denatured alcohol. Rinse and thoroughly dry the washed glass between layers of newspaper. Avoid using paper toweling because it leaves lint and chemical residues on the surfaces.

Photo 6-2
A drape mold can be used to fire a painted single-thick piece of glass. Once fired, the enamel used will be on the underside of the plate.

Photo 6-3
This dragon necklace (pattern on page 57) was outlined and painted with Fuse Master enamels.

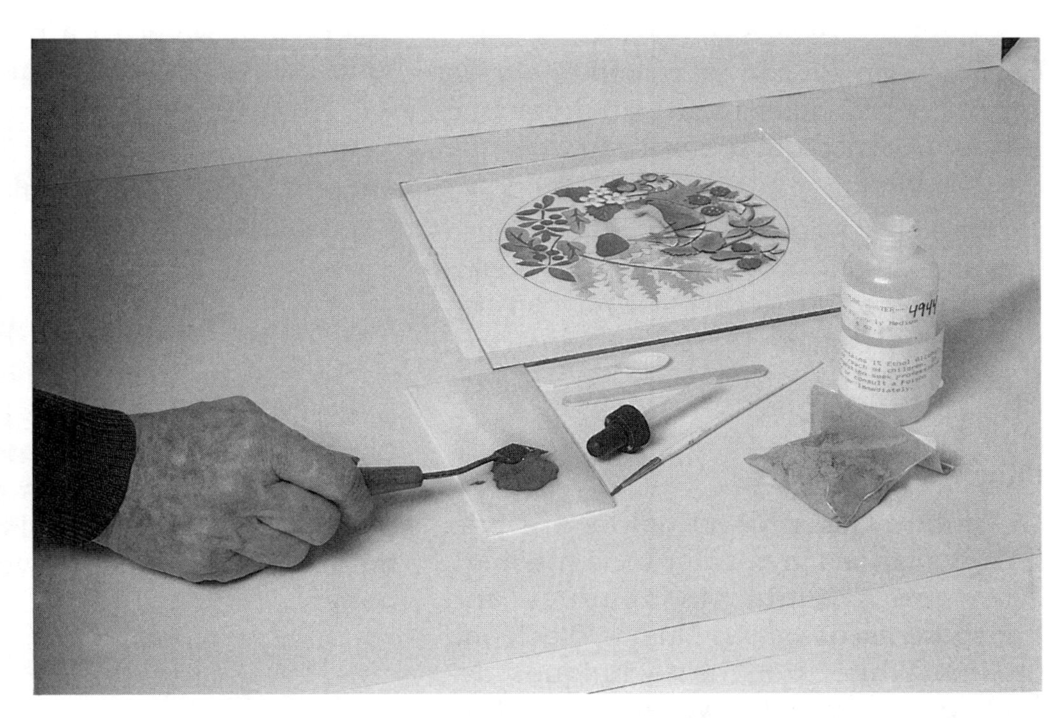

Photo 6-4
A clean piece of glass can serve as a palette for mixing dry enamel powders and liquid.

Mixing Enamels

Fuse Master Enamels

If you are using Fuse Master enamels for the patterns in this book, select the lead-free opaque ones, which are deeper in color than the transparents. (Photo 6-3).

Use a palette knife or mixing stick on a clean piece of glass or use a small jar to mix the enamels according to the following formula. (Photo 6-4).

Formula

- 1/2 teaspoon of opaque enamel, three drops of Water Friendly Medium (by Fusion Headquarters), and 1/2 teaspoon water.
- Stir the Water Friendly Medium and water into the enamel powder until the mixture has a creamy consistency. Stir in two or three more drops of water from an eyedropper if necessary.
- The enamels can be mixed to a variety of consistencies to suit your painting needs. The medium burns away when the glass is fired.

Mixed black liquid enamel can be placed into an extruder bottle and used for outlining (explained in this chapter).You can also use a Magic Outlining Pen (Eastman Corp). (Photo 6-5).

Unique Glass Colors

Unique Glass brand colors are premixed enamels in a water base medium. They are available in opaques and transparents, as well as Outline Black and Outline White. For the techniques described in this chapter, we recommend the opaque enamels.

There are several different categories of Unique opaque colors. All colors within each category can be mixed freely with each other to create endless shades. When fired, the A family colors mature to a bright shiny finish; the B family are matte finished and must be applied thinly; the C family is comprised of earth tones, warm tans, and earth browns; the D family has the brilliant cadmium red, orange and yellow. Although *different color families cannot be mixed together*, a color from one category can be applied on top of a color from another, once the first color has completely dried.

Stirring Unique Enamels

Stir each color well with a palette knife. Colors tend to settle in the jar and have to be stirred before and during use. Thin the colors with water to a milk-like consistency, and use the paint directly from the jar. (Photo 6-6).

If the colors dry out in the jar, add enough water to return them to a painting consistency.

Applying Enamels

To use the paint technique with the patterns provided in this book, trace or photocopy the pattern onto white paper. Use crayons or markers and color the pattern to use as a guide. Place your glass tin side down directly over the colored pattern.

Photo 6-5
The parrot pattern (page 40) is placed under the glass. An extruder bottle is used to outline the design.

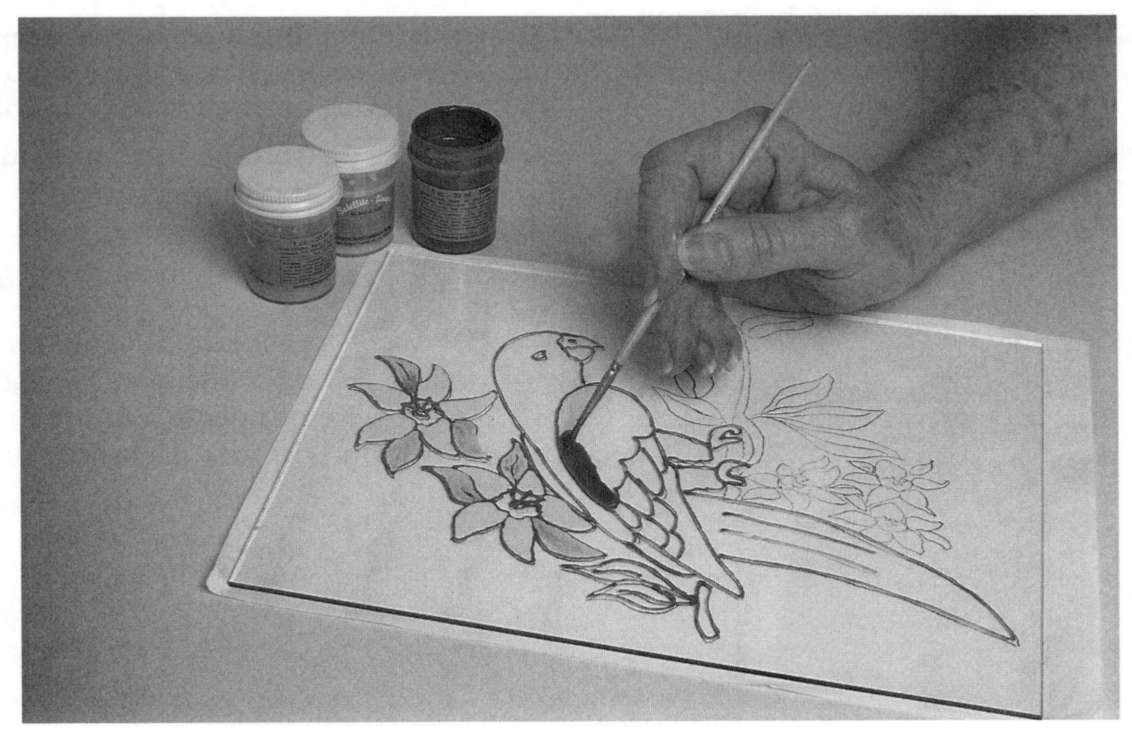

Photo 6-6
Some liquid enamels are ready to use and can be painted directly from the jar. Brush the colored enamels into the areas outlined in black.

Outliners

Black and White Outliners come in a bottle with a pointed metal tip, ideal for outlining designs. Use a fine wire to clean out the tiny hole in the tip. Immerse the tip in water immediately after use.

Using an outline around areas gives more design definition and keeps the colors from running together. Before applying other colors, wait until the outline has dried. (Photo 6-5).

Trace the pattern with the tip of the outliner bottle or an extruder bottle, or use a small round brush with black enamel. When the outliner is dry, "puddle" the colors for a stained glass look. Use a brush to bring the color up to the outlines. (Photo 6-6)

Applying Enamels without an Outline

If you prefer not to use an outliner, allow each color to dry before applying an adjacent color.

- In small areas, puddle the colors on with a soft brush loaded with enamel.
- To cover a large area (background, etc.), you can apply the thinned color with an eye-dropper.
- Tilt the glass to allow brush marks to flow out.

Note: If color is applied too thickly, it may curl and flake when drying or "bead" during firing.

Removing Unwanted Enamel

To remove unwanted enamel after it has been applied to the glass, allow the enamel to dry and remove it with a sharp object such as a pen point, razor, or wooden stick. Gently remove enamel dust or chips with a soft brush, and then reapply the enamel.

Special Effects

After preparation, colors can be sponged, brushed, airbrushed, marbleized, stippled, or stenciled. And colors can be shaded, one color over another.

A gold ceramic pen (with firing capability to 1400°F) can be used to add gold highlights or outlines.

To apply liquid enamels with an airbrush, thin enamel with a few drops of water. Spray on three or four even coats of enamel. If the glass is warmed before spraying, the enamel will dry quickly and will not be as likely to run. (Photo 6-7).

For delicate backgrounds, use a soft sponge to apply the enamel. (Photo 6-8).

Cleaning Up

Wash brushes and outliner tip with water. If the tip becomes clogged, insert a fine wire or needle into the opening. A cleaning wire comes with the outliner bottles.

Photo 6-7
An air brush can be used to apply liquid enamels. Before cutting your stencils, cover them with clear contact paper.

Photo 6-8
Liquid enamels applied with a sponge creates a soft background for this parrot scene.

Parrot Pattern

This pattern is ideal for painting with liquid enamel. First outline the details with black enamel, then paint and shade the parrot and leaves. Sponge on the enamel for a delicate background. Refer to photos 6-5, 6-6, 6-8.

Chapter 7
Safety First

To help you work in a safe and efficient manner and prevent accidents, here are a number of things to remember.

Heat and Fire Safety

❍ Floors and surfaces should be made of fire resistant materials that are easy to mop and sponge clean.

❍ Keep areas around the kiln free of flammable and combustible materials. Sufficient work space should be provided around kilns.

❍ Fire extinguishers or other approved fire control equipment should be installed. Post and practice emergency fire procedures.

❍ Work in a well-ventilated area. Provide kiln with exhaust ventilation such as a canopy hood, or place the kiln near a window exhaust fan.

❍ If you burn yourself, keep the affected area immersed in ice-cold water until the pain diminishes, or wrap an ice cube in a clean cloth and place it on the burned area. If you have a severe burn, call your doctor immediately.

❍ Make sure to have a fire extinguisher nearby in case of a fire.

Protective Clothing

❍ Use safety glasses to protect your eyes when cutting glass.

❍ Use heat-proof gloves when touching the kiln.

❍ To prevent cuts, wear comfortable, non-bulky gloves when working with glass.

❍ Wear a smock or cover-up apron to protect you and your clothing from glass and lead dust. Leave it in the studio. Wash work clothes frequently and separately from other clothes.

❍ Avoid wearing synthetic clothing, loose sleeves, or other items that could melt, burn, or catch fire from radiated heat. Keep clothing and sleeves away from the work surface.

❍ Long hair should be tied back.

Precautions

❍ Spray products containing solvents should be used with local exhaust ventilation.

❍ Never apply enamels in or near living or eating areas.

❍ Do not eat, drink, smoke, or apply makeup while working with glass enamels. Wash hands before eating.

❍ If you are going to be working with glass enamels for an extended time, use a protective mask and an exhaust fan.

❍ Clean up enamel spills immediately. Use wet cleaning methods to avoid raising dust. Do not allow dust to remain on floors to be tracked into other areas.

❍ Glass and enamel grinding dust should be disposed of as toxic waste.

❍ Read and follow manufacturers' instructions and warnings regarding their products. When purchasing chemicals, ask for the Materials Safety Data Sheets that relate to them.

❍ Label all chemicals that have been transferred into new containers.

Handling Glass

❍ Do not grasp large glass sheets by their corners. Instead, hold the glass vertically to keep it from breaking in your hands.

❍ Glass splinters fly, so protect your eyes. Always use safety glasses when cutting or grinding glass.

❍ Use a table brush to keep the work surface free of glass chips.

❍ Do not allow small children into your studio or work area without supervision.

❍ Keep a first-aid kit handy.

Pattern Section

Use the following patterns for stenciling and painting.

Sea Horse

A good beginner stencil pattern that can be used for a plate or panel. The various shades suggest four different colors that could be used. This requires four stencils, one for each color. The two smallest areas shown as black should be sifted first as described in Chapter 3.

Sailboat

A simple stencil pattern for plate or pattern. This pattern can be reduced to create a small suncatcher.

Floral Wreath

An easy stencil pattern for an eight inch plate. Suggestion: Use one flower on a small piece of glass to create a pin.

Butterfly and Angel

Simple stencil patterns for suncatchers.

An easy stencil pattern for plates

Autumn Leaves

A moderately easy stencil for panel or plate.

Bird and Flowers

A moderately easy stencil pattern. Leave out some flowers, if desired. The pattern can be used for a plate or suncatcher.

Aquarium

Intermediate stencil pattern for plate or panel. Use fish individually to create a jewelry pin.

Clown

An intermediate pattern which can be used for plate or panel.

Bird in Dogwood Tree

This pattern can be sifted or painted with enamels. Some experience helpful.

Holly Leaves and Bow

This pattern is for an intermediate skill level. It can be used for a plate or suncatcher.

Victorian Lady

An intermediate pattern which can be sifted or painted for a plate or panel.

Fruit

This pattern is for an intermediate skill level. It is ideal for a plate. Helpful hint: If sifting, apply a small amount of black enamel for seeds on strawberries.

Dragon

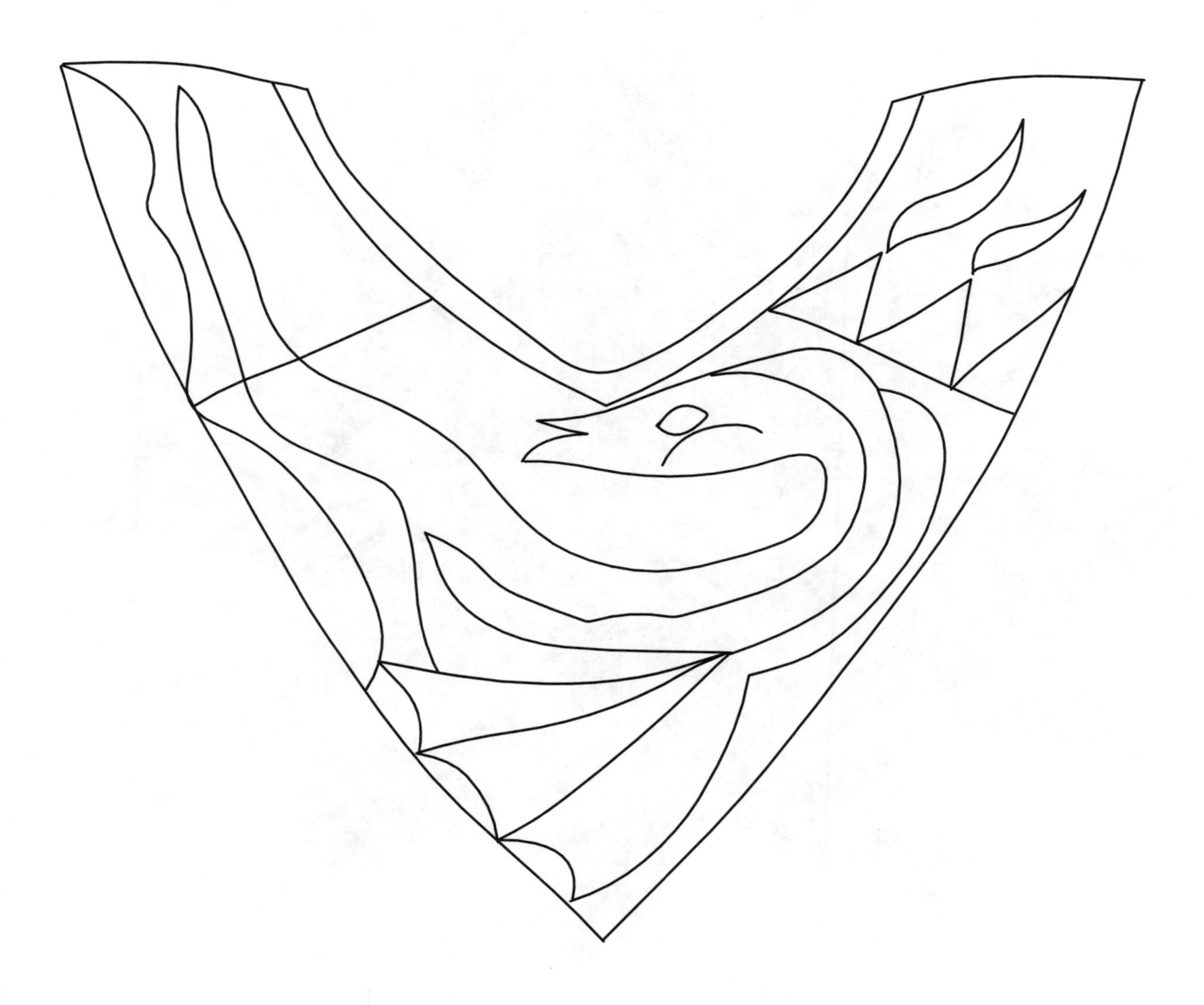

An intermediate pattern to create a plate or jewelry collar. It is ideal for painting. For drama, outline with black first (explained in chapter six).

Poinsettia

Some experience helpful for this plate pattern. It can be dry sifted or painted. Note: If sifting enamels, add center dots last.

Cougar

Ideal pattern for painting. Use for a plate or panel.

Frog

An intermediate pattern which can be sifted or painted. Ideal for a plate or panel.

Reference Section

Book References

Stained Glass
A Guide to Today's Tiffany Copper Foil Technique
by Kay Bain Weiner
Watson-Guptill Publications, New York. 1994

Contemporary Art Glass
by Ray and Lee Grover
Crown Publishers, Inc., New York, 1975

Enchanted Creations
by Fused Fantasies
text by Darlene Johnson and illustrated by Judy Lee
Bradenton, Florida, 1988

Glass Craft
by Kay Kinney
Chilton Books, Philadelphia/New York 1962

Glass Forming
by Keith Cummings
B T Batsford, London, 1975

Glass Fusing
Book One, by Boyce Lundstrom and Daniel Schwoerer
Vitreous Publications, Inc.,1983

The Fused Glass Handbook
by Gil Reynolds
Portland, Oregon 1987

Kiln-Fired Glass
by Harriette Anderson
Chilton Book Company,
Radnor, Pennsylvania, 1970

Kiln-Fired Glass
by Mary Bergsma
Thompson Enamel
Highland Park, Illinois, 1983

The Artist's Complete Health and Safety Guide, Second Edition
by Monona Rossol
1996

Manufacturers and Suppliers

Listed below are some of the manufacturers and suppliers of tools and material mentioned in this book. Although some manufacturers do not sell directly to the consumer, they may be able to direct you to a local supplier of a specific item. Call the suppliers listed below for more information.

Ceramic Supply of New York and New Jersey, Inc.
534 La Guardia Place
New York, New York 10012
(212) 475-7236

7 Route 46 West
Lodi, New Jersey 07644
(201) 340-3005
(Plate stackers, kilns, kiln gloves, kiln serparators)

Eastman Corporation
P.O. Box 247
Roselle, New Jersey 07203
(908) 232-1212
(Magic Outlining pens)

Fletcher Terry Company
65 Spring Lane
Farmington, Connecticut 06032
(800) 843-3826
(Oval & circle glass cutters, glass cutters, pliers)

Fusion Headquarters, Inc.
P.O. Box 69312
Portland, Oregon 97201
(503) 245-7547
(Enamels, overglaze, molds, kilns and supplies)

Jen-Ken Kilns
3615 Ventura Drive W.
Lakeland, Florida 33811
(800) 329-5456
(Kilns, accessories)

Thompson Enamel
P.O. Box 310
Newport, Kentucky 41072
(800) 545-2776
(Enamels, sifters)

Unique Glass Colors
Drawer 20
Logansport, Louisiana 71049
(318) 697-2611
(Liquid enamels, molds)

About the Author

Kay Bain Weiner teaches workshops throughout the United States and abroad. She won the Award for Best Instructor '95 from the Stained Glass Industry. She is the author of books and publications and is a frequent contributor to several stained glass magazines including *Glass Art, Glass Patterns Quarterly,* and *Glass Artist Magazine.* She has been the coordinator of the National Glass Craft Conference for eight years.

Other Books and Tapes by Kay Bain Weiner

Stained Glass
A Guide to Today's Tiffany Copper Foil Techniques
Watson-Guptil Publishers

Stained Glass Magic Book
Chilton Publishers

From Eastman Publishers

Brush on Color Magic

In Your Wildest Imagination

Solder Magic Book - Patterns and Instructions

More Solder Magic

Baubles, Dangles & Beads - Stained Glass Jewelry Book

Line & Color Magic for Glass Design Book

Tapes

Create with Color Magic Stains (Video Tape)

Solder Magic (Video Tape)

Creativity & Color for Glass Design (Audio Tapes)